EXPRESS

*Express Express Expres*

UNIVERSITY OF PITTSBURGH PRESS

# Express Express **Express**

## *James Reiss*

Published by the University of Pittsburgh Press, Pittsburgh, Pa. 15260
Copyright © 1983, James Reiss
All rights reserved
Feffer and Simons, Inc., London
Manufactured in the United States of America

**Library of Congress Cataloging in Publication Data**

Reiss, James.
    Express.

    (Pitt poetry series)
    I. Title.
PS3568.E52E9    1983        811'.54        82-13504
ISBN 0-8229-3474-4
ISBN 0-8229-5346-3 (pbk.)

Acknowledgment is made to the following publications for permission to re-print some of the poems that appear in this book: *The American Poetry Review, The Kenyon Review, New York Times,* and *The Virginia Quarterly Review.*

"Arigato Means Thank You," © 1977 by James Reiss, first appeared in *American Review #26,* published by Bantam Books, Inc. "A Candy Store in Washington Heights," "God Knows Many Stories," and "The Ohio Massacre" were first published in *Antaeus.* "Leaving" first appeared in *The Antioch Review,* Vol. 34, No. 3 (Spring 1976). "Palisades Amusement Park" originally appeared in *Argo.* "A Day in Ohio" and "Things to Remember" were first published in *Esquire* magazine. "Anna's Song" and "Schilfgraben" first appeared in *The Hudson Review.* "The Mittenleaf Tree" first appeared in *The Iowa Review,* Vol. 10, No. 2, and is used with permission. "Cindy" and "The Escape of the Convict" were originally published in *The Nation.* "Approaching Washington Heights," "By the Steps of the Metropolitan Museum of Art," "Passage," and "Sueños" appeared originally in *The New Yorker.* "Good-bye to the Diamond," © 1980 *The Niagara Magazine,* is published by permission. "Brothers" first appeared in *The Ohio Review.* "On Learning the People's Republic of China Has Lifted Its Ban on Beethoven" was originally published in *Poetry.* "Elegy for Jay Silverheels" first appeared in *Southwest Review.*

The author also wishes to thank: Creative Artists Public Service (CAPS), the National Endowment for the Arts, the MacDowell Colony, Miami University's Faculty Research Committee, and the Ohio Arts Council.

Special thanks to Barbara Eve and Philip Schultz.

*The publication of this book is supported by grants
from the National Endowment for the Arts
in Washington, D.C., a Federal agency,
and the Pennsylvania Council on the Arts.*

For my mother

# CONTENTS

# CONTENTS

# One Two Three Four Five

# APPROACHING WASHINGTON HEIGHTS

North, near the tip, where the island
raises its head like a factory
worker who has been asleep in a gray cap
and who blinks, his eyes full of sand
his lips chapped with age

where the only bridge in America
that can sing "Ol' Man River" with the wind
in its cables has an audience of fire
escapes, and the brown ledge
of the land sprouts names
like Chittenden Avenue, Cabrini Boulevard

I who have driven three decades of A trains
shotgun to the motorman from midtown
glued to the window
as we highballed sixty blocks without a stop
up the guts of an electric eel

north past stray stations, dimwatted
mudugly, platforms
that would be the rust-colored scenarios
of nightmares in which I would race
to catch a train but never make it
my legs churning in the same spot

I who am churning now, who have stayed
on, not gotten off pale-faced
in Harlem as if in the middle of a sentence

I who will never get off this train
of thought, these silver wheels
                              barreling
north toward the black mammoth elevators
and hammering escalators of 181st Street

where the man who sells tokens has a life
behind bars totally alien
from mine, though his face is also a map
of Israel, his eyes are tiny
dead seas

# A CANDY STORE
# IN WASHINGTON HEIGHTS

One of those two-bit luncheonettes on a nothing
block with Coca-Cola
signs and an owner who looks like Groucho Marx.
One of those holes in the heat
wall of summer
up the hill from the bridge and its lighthouse.
One of those prewar leftovers
that specialize in Hamilton Beach malted mixers
and fans on the ceiling
where BLTs were always
a quarter and the owner, Levine, still stoops
with a cigar that has been rotting
in his hand for thirty years.

> *Levine of the gray suspenders,*
> *Levine of the white shirt in summer that is always fading,*
> *Levine of the brown teeth and baldspot, scooping ice cream*
> *    from your old horse of a freezer:*

By the magazine rack,
by the blackening collection of comics
and dustmice, a boy who has paid for his malted
with his palms up, letting
you dip for dimes,
has his nose in Wonder Woman.
Today he will sneak it under his T-shirt.
While you are screwing the ketchup
or cursing the Germans,
he will slink out the door
                              with the turn
of your cheek.

Locked in his bedroom
for hours, he will pore over "Wonder
Woman in Jersey City," "Batman
Trapped in the Cave of Lost Guano"—
and will rise to his mother's
shouts for dinner only when the scraps
of paper on his desk tell everything
he knows about bridges in sunlight.

> *Levine of the frankfurter fingers,*
> *Levine of the dishrag and dills,*
> *Levine of the Life Savers, Charms, the small cherry Cokes*
> *    that are never enough:*

In one of those dustbins
swept up from the gutters of streets
not far from the river that summer,
I stole the cigar from your mouth
and the hundred wads of Chiclets
stuck under your counter.

I stuffed them under my T-shirt.
I kneaded them in my pocket.
I shaped them into a bridge.
I sat at my desk as I shaped
the sun-silver towers, the roadway,
the lighthouse red as a matchtip—
for you, Levine, for you.

*One Two Three Four Five*

# SUEÑOS

In my dreams I always speak Spanish.
The cemetery may be in Brooklyn,
and I may be kneeling on a rise
looking out at the skyline of the city,
but I will whisper, *Mira el sol.*

And it is true the late morning
sun will turn that bank of skyscrapers
the color of bleached bone in Sonora,
and all the window washers of Manhattan
will white-out like a TV screen

in Venezuela turning to snow.
But the gray face on the headstone photograph
has a nose like my father's,
and his voice had the lilt of the ghettos
of central Europe.

So I should kneel lower and say something
in Yiddish about fathers, grandfathers,
the hacked limbs of a family tree
that reaches as high as Manhattan.
I should say, *Grampa, I loved those times*

*we ran through the underpasses in Central
Park, you with your cane, I with my ice
cream cones, shouting for echoes,
bursting out into sunlight—*
if I only knew the language to say it in.

# THINGS TO REMEMBER

that the man stooped over his desk
all day in an office with gray
wallpaper has a pocket
watch his grandfather gave him
on a park bench

that once in a park
a row of green benches
was mottled with sun under a network
of ivy

that the old man reaching deep
in his pocket
unfolded something
the boy had never seen, larger
than a silver dollar

that the boy slid
off the bench, leaped in circles
with the watch dangling on its chain
and begged him to snap it open

whereupon the boy pressed it to his ear
like a seashell, sighing and circling
to an invisible victrola of drumtaps

# ORANGE ICE

A green-slatted bench under a mulberry tree, sticky
in the heat and jelly of June: Once after supper
—thirsty, fingernail-dirty—I pedaled a sidewalk
to park my trike by a carved-rock water fountain,
stone-dry, broken, and yell for you, Grandma.
From your bench you rose and bought me my first orange ice.
But the color of twilight froze on my tongue,
and I said nothing.

Now I say thanks to your pillows at home
for smelling like stale pastry.
Thanks to the quilt stitched by your sister
which looked like the Austro-Hungarian Empire.
I napped on top of your raggedy blankets and dreamed
of Grandpa waiting on tables, balancing trays
of whipped cream on his wedding ring—
until, bandy-legged, he crashed
into a maitre d' and took up dishwashing.

Far from your widow's sink in Sheepshead Bay
where teaspoons swam in a glass like dentures,
a continent careening down the path
to darkness ground its teeth—
and your sister groaned, your brother's ashes rose
in rice-white puffs from a chimney.

Yet you suffered my war whoops at sundown
up three flights of stairs
and ran a shower for me, unaware.
Your ignorant hands turned the knobs,
and orange water froze from the nozzle
into twin cylinders fused together, dripping
in the steam and syrup of June.

# BROTHERS

Eighteen years you beat me over the head
with the butt end of our brotherhood.
So where are you now, Mr. Top
Dog on the Bunk Bed, Mr. Big
Back on the High School Football Team?

You hauled ass out of that town
with its flimsy goalposts.
Now you're down there with your Dead
Sea, your Jerusalem, busy
with the same old border disputes

that sparked our earliest fist fights.
Israel is just another locked toy
closet on your side of the bedroom, split
by electric train tracks. It's as if
you never left home at all: Yesterday

in a bar in Washington Heights
I saw a man who could have been you.
The Jets were playing the Steelers with two
downs to go, and in the icy
lightshow of smoke

he lifted a pitcher of beer
and swilled it just as the screen
blazed red with an ad for Gillette.
And I thought, Here is my blood brother
whose only gifts to me were kicks

in the teeth, his cast-off comic books,
and worst of all, wrapped, sharpened
for a lifetime,
the perfect razor of my rage.

# PALISADES AMUSEMENT PARK (1897–1971)

The world's largest electric billboard
bright enough to read across a milewide river
once sparked drivers on the Henry Hudson Parkway,
casting silver spells on the water
like advertisements for the moon.
Perched atop traprock cliffs, that billboard said:

"Come all you New Yorkers with unamusing lives.
Travel the bridge that looks like a rhinestone necklace.
When you reach the tollbooth of exact change
give it all you have and bear left
for the Whip and the Cyclone.

I am the fat lady in funhouse mirrors.
I am the fortune teller with the lisp
who predicts early fame and white Cadillacs.
I am the bumper cars and the guy
who sells popcorn by the Caterpillar
with plenty of rancid butter and salt."

# GOOD-BYE TO THE DIAMOND

Who on the parapet
of an old fort by a river
can resist the tinkle of xylophones
when a breeze lifts the kellygreen skirts
of hundredyear oaks
loaded with blackthroated sparrows?

And who on mosstriggered gun emplacements
can ignore the revolutionary
war of tulip and daffodil
in formal gardens shot by the onagain offagain sun?

I had been wandering all morning between the blue
and yellow umbrella of the hot dog vender
and a flower bed my mother pointed
out to me when I was still in my stroller:
*Candytuft,* she explained over and over
pointing to the white cluster
till I could taste a cotton candy mash
of sugarcoated petals.

Once uniformed park attendants loitered
hooking their boots through wrought iron dividers
at the edge of a dandelion patch
where I tripled and homered
onto Riverside Drive.

Now I paused at Washington's Flagpole and said good-bye
to the diamond, good-bye to the crabgrass
and peashooters, to the legions
of whitestockinged nannies wheeling carriages
past beds of baby's breath.

# A DAY IN OHIO

The painters began work on the house,
wielding their brushes like wings.
By noon they took off their caps
and blotted their brows with tan rags,
then lit cigarettes by striking wooden
matches on their boots in long slow arcs.

The roof took on the color of the sun
as it broke yolklike on the weather vane.
They did not see it splatter.
Bronze in their five-o'clock shadows,
they slapped one last gold stroke
and lowered their scaffold and stretched.

# THE OHIO MASSACRE

The convention of sweethearts
is meeting in the chandelier ballroom
of the Buckeye Hotel—which is why
I must find the air conditioning
and crawl through dark silver
ducts until I emerge above the delegates
who are scribbling notes to each other
with lipstick, fumbling for phrases,
and bashfully blowing their noses.

I must whip out my switchblade and wait
for the unfurling of the Banner
of Love; then, just as it arcs, heart-
shaped into view, I must cut the cord
and watch the chandelier crash
on all the soft heads and friendly faces
I have lived among for years.

# THE ESCAPE OF THE CONVICT

As dawn broke over Frog Mountain
the police dogs sprang from their kennels
of straw and lost themselves in the glassy
rills at the base of slate cliffs.
By now he had peeled off his striped
uniform and arrived at a shack
near tree line dressed in work
clothes left by the Resistance.

The shack glared on the slope
like a mirror among pine needles,
and the pond's eye winked in the blue
spruce like a woman he had known
all his life but had never, somehow,
touched with a white zeal.

# WILLOW AVENUE

Three white picket fences cross my view:
one for my dooryard, one for my landlord's lawn.
I circle the carpet all day in my rented room
because I have come to distrust these maples
and marigolds, because the third picket fence
across the street is opening, yes, as my neighbor
approaches his mailbox, his face a haze.

In his golf shirt and shorts
he cannot see me here behind the drapes.
He leaves his letter, lifts a red steel flag,
and hobbles back to his front porch,
betraying any manner of grace
with his ungainly walking stick.

I have stumbled around myself long enough to know
I, too, have betrayed my ambition.
I have not written a word or raked the leaves
of the hackberry tree by the breezeway.
So what if their slippery pulp spoils the path.
So what if, high in the branches,
their witches'-brooms drop fungus.

These rooms where mildew makes its home,
these clapboard colonials,
have given themselves up to orchards
of boredom and abandoned railway crossings
where the roadbed sags under creosote ties.

## LEAVING

Where was I that day I gazed
down a tree-lined street that dead-ended
in hayfields?
There was no wind, and leaves
drooped over white frame houses like hands

limp with heat.
It might have been a side street on Cape Cod
on the most desolate Wednesday
if not for the hayfields.
If not for the houses

it might have been a road in ancient Canaan
where I might have been standing stock-
still, bearing the genes of my future,
the face of a stranger,
like a branch in my hand.

As I started to town with my suitcase
the afternoon darkened with starlings.
And when I arrived at the station
a cloudburst of twittering beaks
had hit the trees and raised the roof

of such a greenhouse of hot air
that the street was ablaze with jet
feathers, black Japanese fans
flapping open at twilight, at home
in their filth-spattered nests.

# GOD KNOWS MANY STORIES

This morning walking to work
I thought of silos in South Dakota.
It would be earlier out west.
That grower of roses, the dawn,
would be doing his work while the wheat fields

would be whispering their usual suicide
notes to the wind. Here, too, as usual the Empire
State Building was a hypodermic needle
plunged into God's blue eye.
Where had I heard that expression God's

blue eye, I asked myself. In South Dakota?
I had never been there, never been west
of the Hudson. Then why
was I thinking of silos
till my ears rang with the swoosh

of grain being sprayed from huge hoses
into elevators, white towers?
I entered my building and went up God knows
many stories to an office with plate
glass windows that gave

on a harvest of workers
whipped by the wind from New Jersey.
There was no smog; the sky was cobalt blue.
Everywhere skyscraper silos
tore into view.

# BY THE STEPS OF THE
# METROPOLITAN MUSEUM OF ART

—for Thomas Lux

Choking with silent laughter, the chalk-faced mime
jousts with the crowd, grabs a smiling sailor,
and sets him on his knees before a school-
girl posed with a rose in her teeth.
The crowd explodes, and the air
is charged with the jingle of loose change.

A driver waiting for the light to change
pulls to the curb and tosses the mime
a silver coin that glitters in midair
before dropping at the feet of the sailor,
making him smile more widely and show his teeth
like a politician visiting a high school.

I drift and think of a dancing school
I drove my daughters to. I watched them change
into shy swans, gifted to the teeth
with graceful napes and wrists—just as the mime
is graceful in his placement of the sailor
whose smile unwinds in the afternoon air

when all at once an air-
raid siren I haven't heard since public school
starts shrieking from some roof. The sailor
takes off with the pigeons, unsmiling for a change.
The schoolgirl puts fingers in her ears. The mime
pretends he's screaming, gritting his teeth.

It is like fingernails down chalkboards setting teeth
on edge, this siren slicing the air.
People scatter. Even the mime
slinks uptown, and the school-
girl disappears without her rose—as if she could change
my image of her with the sailor

**21**

at her feet, that skittery peacoated sailor,
both blushing red as the rose in her teeth,
posed statuelike without change. . . .
I leave the museum to escape the air-
raid siren. Up the street school
buses idle, double-parked, and I notice the mime,

the chalk-faced mime, outside my daughters' school
in the three-o'clock air. He lists like a sailor,
whistles through his teeth, and begs for change.

# NEW YORK IS MY CITY

Here where the wind from New Jersey
dumps buckets of ice on the skin
of the river and rooftop clotheslines bell
like flags in a schoolyard
of shouters punchball players and girls
skipping rope to a silent count

where every cobblestone that brightens
in the sun confirms my grandparents' belief
these streets are paved with gold
and chalk marks on the sidewalk spell
hopscotch in any language

I am king of the hill
hoisted shoulder-high over 181st Street
by every aproned butcher and candystore man
every loose-footed elevator operator
out of work in a neighborhood
of six-story walkups

Here where merely to walk down
to the river is an experience
etched in azure never gray
the Palisades shoot up in their leather jacket
of sunlight and frame a painting

of a boy hefted by sweat-spangled elders
who arrived in this city on ships
in rag shirts and European shoes
and made the sidewalks leap to meet their feet
that now tramp riverward
past their fishstores and fruitstands

Here where the tarred and feathery land
dips to a ballfield a tarmac
under the struts of a steel suspension bridge
I am lifted seaward flying
over the heads of the elders who have borne

the burden of my youth smiling and only now
when I am halfway to the heights
of moon mountains toss up their caps
in a geyser that reaches
Lake Tear of the Clouds

# One Two Three Four Five ⟶

# ARIGATO MEANS THANK YOU

This morning I woke with the word
*arigato* on my lips.
                              Was it Japanese?
I lay by you in a sauna
bath of sun and wondered why *arigato*
instead of *breasts* or *silence*.
I had never loved language
more than the night I learned your breasts
were vessels of silence.
                              Still,
I would never dream of saying things
like *Will you have saki, darling?*
I had certainly never taken a course
in foreign correspondences or the exotic
marriage of orange and gold possible
through sunny curtains.
                              Yet here I lay
on a brightening plain, saying
*arigato* over and over
                              until you
slid out of your pale kimono
of sleep and spoke to me in many tongues.

# ANANDI

smoothes her mat on the floor and does her Sun Salute
with arms spread-eagled and the look of joy
Krishna must have worn when he first saw the dawn
sun carried in oxcarts between snowy Himalayan peaks
and the green pearl of Ceylon. How many miles
his vista comprehended she now knows,
who crouches and does push-ups to honor the astral
flames inside her, all around her.
She is a tungsten filament candescent
in our winter-dark living room.

Why should I desecrate her morning prayer?
I never loved darkness. When I was a child
I needed a screen by my bed to prevent me from seeing
the blackness of a hall without a night-light.
I need the sun to lift me from a sleep,
to carry me in a chariot beyond expectation.
So why should I expect
her to remain in the shade of atheism
or put on a shawl and pray to Jehovah?

She'd rather give her energy to One
whose luminescence veils her face.
She does a deep knee bend, and her saffron
robe gathers folds, rippling in the manner of Italian
Renaissance paintings of saints awaiting angels.
Yet she chants in Sanskrit about a paradise
for Brahmans and Untouchables.

She touches my root of skepticism, my core of pride,
my wooden opinions on ethics and sex.
As a pond in the Berkshires lures
the outline of Mount Everest, its crags
and crevasses superimposed over mirroring waves,
she leads me
to the perfumed water of her bath,
disrobing slowly, exposing
her shoulders and breasts, tiny Taj Mahals.

# WHOLE HOURS OF US

Time and again when I entered you I felt
fire up my spine, that frail hook-and-ladder.
I felt like a landlord ransacking his rooms
with a flashlight and gas can.
Oh, I was the fireman's helmet
and the siren's red eye rolled into one

while you, poor you, were the innocent victim of men
who played arson with the littered
back stairways of your feelings.
The catwalks of your nerve ends were kissed
by flaming tongues—your quaint bulk shuddered
and sighed—yet I felt your complicity
in this, our only recourse.
I felt you enter me, evicting guilt.

# THE MITTENLEAF TREE

Then he hid behind the tree
and showed her his gizmo.
But she looked elsewhere; she
gazed over the lake
at the fire-blackened hotel

where men were already busy
repairing the dock—
she could almost smell the fresh
two-by-fours and taste paint
remover on her breath.

Then while he was skinny-dipping
behind a rock
she grabbed his blue bermudas
and one red sneaker
and sprinted up the trail.

Well, I've been wondering all these years
what's become of them: is he a clerk
or spot welder? And what about her
toothpick legs? We all know
dry wood snaps.

But what if she is a ballerina
as she wished, and he
is a neurosurgeon? Does this
make them happy?
I'd like to think of them smiling

over margaritas, not split
by a thousand miles.
I'd like to think of them elsewhere,
making love under a quilt
of mitten-shaped leaves by a lake

with bullfrogs like wolf whistles
and, hammering in the distance, workers
who straddle the August shore
as a glove
straddles all five fingers.

# DRIVING MY DAUGHTER TO CAMP

The bumblebee on Paddington Bear
that stung you on the stomach
and made you howl in the back seat
now is ground into the cinder
shoulder along Route 6.

If you had met him somewhere
in a sunny field by a stable,
you might have loved his buzzing
and listened to it long
after the counselors unsaddled the horses.
You might have wanted to fly
with him home to his hive.

Now you are away your tenth summer,
stumbling into boys, bumping
into menstruation and your own new breasts
in a bathhouse mirror.

May a boyfriend bring you candy:
fudge from Godiva's, licorice.
Not a love bite that leaves you bruised.
Not the sting of bitterness, my sweet.

# CINDY

The dustmice skittered all night
under the trundle bed,
but when she looked in the morning
they had escaped through the floorboards,
shedding gray clots of fur, damp skins
of grit like steel wool.

Then why was it they always returned
with the click of a light switch
on squeaky invisible feet?
And why was her mother never
there when the Grandfather of Dustmice
crept from his knothole at midnight,
immense as an onion?

She would lie alone, not close
her eyes for a minute,
while he skittered in the corner,
chattering through his fangs
that he was her only friend.

# ELEGY FOR JAY SILVERHEELS (1920–1980)

The night the Lone Ranger got shot and you leaped onto the screen
lithe as a wildcat in black-and-white TV buckskin with tomahawk
I had just that day learned the word *tonto* in Spanish means stupid.
Class had let out, and I thought,
So this is what they call you for helping a good guy,
tripping up crooks in a grownup schoolyard.
Now I am grownup and finger the silver
bullet of my accomplishments as a poor excuse for another person's hand.
I gallop to do good, I jog to capture a sunrise,
and as sure as whitewall tires line a side street I am a masked man.

If only I could throw off this sadness, my heavy headdress,
and build a fire and smoke a pipe for our ancestors
who rode this planet's saddle side by side:
sidekicks with winged heels,
they were stupid, they shot for the sun.

# TRYING NOT TO FEEL DESPERATE

I try to think of a ranch in Nevada.
I would be happy with an ax and woodstove,
with a view of the Smoke Creek Desert.

If only I could shake out my head and sweep the debris
down over the stoop to be dust with the sagebrush.
If only I could throw away every chipped dish
and subsist on original hardtack.

But even truckers in Reno know
there's more to being stuck than sand
and the smell of burning rubber.

Coyotes know about leaving tracks:
how easy it is to double back
or quench a scent in a flooded arroyo.
They forage in ever-green patterns.
The most I can hope for is an occasional moon
and the moment to howl my head off.

# PUMAS

A woman in a mauve dress mentions
her passion for pumas
I nod gravely and say
I saw a puma cross

outside my window once
years ago holed-up at a writers' colony
Out of the woods it stalked through the snow
pausing to lift each paw

Then topics shift
We move toward the bar and branch off
in separate directions

Later I wonder what she meant
If I who never saw a puma
or anything that winter but my bloated self
crouching in an outhouse mirror
was capable of such snowy untruth
what veils her words must also wear

# SCHILFGRABEN

is German for "reedy ditch." I read it yesterday
on a plaque under a painting of marshland.
When I reached the top of the spiral-tiered gallery,
I stared six stories down at a fountain jetting
and thought of particulars, the proper
names for ferns and vine-hungry moths.

I make a wish for Clara whose hair was straw-yellow.
In my journal one summer I called her "my willowy reed."
I wrote: "Clara's waist-long hair made me feel
like Rilke beside her today as we hiked down a slope
toward the Danube over swampy areas
locally known as The Sedge."

Not one straw-yellow strand lasts, saved
between the pages of my journal, to tell me
she is more than the hollow stalk of a phrase.
Yet I wrote: "She wore a barrette
and braided the dough she baked
in ovens that made me think of Treblinka."

I think of half-tracks, tanks,
the dominance of one idea
without regard for particulars.
Then I imagine Clara hatless in 1980,
leaning over a rolling pin or pounding
dough with her fists.

Shy as a marsh bird, mired behind a counter,
she bags pumpernickel, rye,
says *Auf Wiedersehen* to a customer,
and scribbles on a pad: "These tablespoons,
these numbered measuring cups,
dole out the bread of life."

One Two Three **Four** Five

# EXPRESS

**Younger Son**

In the indigo night-light of a Pullman roomette
I climb down from my tangle-blanketed berth
to sun in the glow from the bulb.
I bathe in a bucket of color. Ultraviolet
in the washroom mirror, I whisper
I am Little Boy Blue—
until, inches away in your lower berth,
you mumble through your mustache, Back to bed.

I check the porter's door for shined shoes,
then climb out of my slippers,
thinking, The sheep's in the meadow—
while the wheels' iambic clack
and the steam engine's whistle
doppler in the ears of drivers
caught at crossings as bells clang red
outside the plate-glass window where you lie.

I dream you stare at vineyards spinning past
until you merge with the Mohawk River Valley,
enveloping grape-grown hills
with one expansive sweep of your arm.
Wine-blue over woolly shadows
of silos in the rain,
you balance track and train on your pajama sleeve
and rock them like a baby.

Swaddled in fog, I am your second son
counting cows in the corn, the river's willows,
while lamps from farmers' parlors glint.
It is four A.M. when you hold me
closer to your vintage breath to mouthe
a lullaby: fish and lumber, coal and hay,
two hundred miles on the Erie Canal—
until morning finds us in a polychrome city.

### Father

Yes, morning found us mostly sunny and mild.
When you grabbed my hand in a taxi
and said, "Look at the Eastman Kodak buildings, Dad,"
I felt as though I'd never seen a skyline: The mist
from Genesee Falls rainbowed,
and the glint off Kodak's red-brick compound
hit me so hard I felt giddy
and overtipped our driver.

I'd known mornings at home by the window
when the river winked through coal
smoke from the Hudson Line
so invitingly I'd wanted to drop my portfolio
and cancel my appointments.
In chiaroscuro New York
I'd photographed "Empire Shade" and "Umber Cathedral."
How could I know Rochester would be rain-washed
        and resplendent?

We leaned on a breeze and made haste
to a conference room where a buyer
sat for our sales show of travel scenes.
But while you fidgeted beside me at the table
that faced a photomural of palm trees and sand dunes,
I thought, For all the lushness of our love—
how I bloomed for you, my second son—
I was a spiny cactus for your brother.

Him I adored until his mother's kiss
found me jealous, hateful.
Hospitalized with asthma the day he graduated kindergarten,
I lay in an oxygen tent,
dreaming my Brownie stills burned in their albums.
Your brother's baby pictures curled aflame.
His bonnet bulged, his crib and diapers crisped
in the incandescent air.

### Older Son

Yet I survived without skin grafts
or curses for your bad moods, Father. Spite
was your woodshed—no whipping post but a week
of silence at the desk or dinner table.
You greeted me with frosty glares that made
your mustache and chinless jaw
look like a painting of Satan
in a book I'd begun.

I read a hundred books, but none expressed
my feelings, none aroused my ire so much
as two words, "darkness visible": The room in the basement
where you developed negatives in hypo,
panning under a red bulb,
was an inferno of stillborn faces
munching Uneeda Biscuits
or brushing with Ipana Toothpaste.

Hung up to dry, your shots of smiles,
your tinted vistas of clouds for American Airlines,
mocked any love you might have wished to express.
Yet you emerged in the clear yellow light
of the kitchen and put your arm around my brother's shoulder.
You took him on business trips while I hung back
or played jazz that lifted me high off the piano stool
to a Jerusalem of pure feeling.

Now I quicken in a duplex with a view
of the Arab Quarter: My window overlooks
a stretch of desert tenanted by Moslems.
I shop in bazaars where veiled women scorn cameras,
selling hummus and falafel to my wife and children.
I stare west between the Suez Canal
and Italy's boot—seven thousand miles—until
I conjure your face, sky-blue in rigor mortis,
and kiss the frozen shutters of your eyelids.

# PROFESSOR WARREN BATES

### 1

A towheaded boy is grinning under an apple tree
with his grandparents. He's wearing shorts.
They're wearing Sears-Roebuck clothes of the 1940s.
They're farmers with plenty of pork
chops and potatoes for the boy,
who seems to grow ganglier every second.

Basketballs sprouted from his hands,
so he balanced them on bitten fingernails.
He tossed balls nervously through a hoop on the apple tree
every day when the river was visible
in winter. He noticed the elms
shielded the river most in June when school let out
and the fish cried, Come and get us.
It felt like playing hooky at first:
The buses vanished, along with the truant officer,
and the roads were free and clear enough to sleep on.
But by August when he'd heard too much of pigs squealing
and Aunt Pearl nitpicking,
he prayed for a speedier means of escape
than his fat-tired Schwinn.

                    On Sunday mornings his prayers
were answered by families flailing and shrieking in tongues
he began to decipher. He studied their shrill hallelujahs
till he could toss them through a hoop of speculation.
He dreamed a rattlesnake slid down his arm, raising the new
hair on his chest. He coiled the snake into a ball
and bounced it into a basket made of straw
next to a wooden flute and an Indian charmer.

**2**

"I stood on a ghat in Benares with my new wife
and thought: It's a long way to Grand Rapids,
yet these robed bathers laying on hands,
laving one another's arms with this polluted river,
share one thing with the suited
wallowers in Christ: They understand filth.
That night on the farm I understood
Grandma and Grandpa were slaughtering a pig in the barn
when they shouted and sent me back to bed.
Even so the smell of pig's blood reached me here
in Benares, and I thought I would retch for the spill,
the loss of liquid more precious than Olympic gold.
I turned to my wife and said,
'Nobody's fat in India, not like Indiana.'
I took out my camera and snapped the cupped
hands and raised arms bathing—no pushing or shoving,
no fighting in line.
My shutter caught a young girl covered with flies
as she reached the water's edge—swish—and splashed
through its net."

**3**

Sunday mornings on the sleeping porch
he rises late to grade student papers
next door to a buckeye tree with a hoop.
He shoots baskets with his son twice a week,
content with custody of his kids, and rumored
to be working on a novel.
I know nothing about novels. I know only
what he tells me by his fireplace.
"They cut the apple tree down," he told me once.
"One day when I stayed home from school
they came with a crosscut saw.
My fever shot so high that afternoon
I went into convulsions,
obsessed with that scene in the barn:
The pig strung up by his legs
was my runaway father squealing.
'Cut him down,' I shrieked,
'and save his blood in a bucket, a basket
of forbidden fruit.'"

# NIXON

### 1

The sweat beaded through his makeup,
and we saw he was nervous about something we would never
      fathom.
When he turned to face Kennedy, the camera caught
a five-o'clock shadow that belied everything he said,
jawboning about toughness, nuclear muscle.
The clock on the studio wall might have ticked backward.
The spotlights might have trained on an earlier rebuttal.
Presto: He is poised over a podium
in his high-school gym, debating the ethics of sex
with a sophomore whose librarian's hairdo
suggests her point of view.
"We should consider sex not only as procreation," he says,
"but as something worth dying for."
He steps down to polite applause, but even the gym
teacher snickers and elbows the assistant coach:
"Ha! That guy's gotta be kidding. What's
his name again?"

### 2

The standard joke about his middle name
was that it was Miltown. Those were tranquil days
when everyone had a checkered career. Khruschev growled
      about peaceful
coexistence one minute, then took off his shoe
and slammed it down on a baize-covered desk,
while we listened on car radios
or paused over pretzels and watched on TV,
less struck by the crazy Russian bear
than the straight man in the Brooks Brothers suit.
He was there like a brand name, entitled to such exposure
because of his special endowment, a stiff upper lip.

**48**

**3**

Somewhere between Whittier and Washington
he began to develop bad posture and look like Howdy
Doody, though he had no freckles
and his chin did not pop up and down on a string.
He was nobody's puppet. The little shaver
had been a Navy man who tasted sea
spray till it chapped his lips and blew holes in his theories.
Indeed, it was the sea that brought him out
of his shell: During sentry duty on deck
one night he had felt something drop from his uniform
and bent with a flashlight.
It might have been the dizzies from the salt air
that hit him—he wasn't sure.
The only thing he knew was that it looked
like a husk or shell. But when he turned it over
all he could remember before fainting was touching
a masklike rubber duplicate of his face.

**4**

Let us assume two parties are vying to buy the Dodge mansion
on Fifth Avenue: Would you side
with those who would keep the property intact
as an aviary and a landmark? Or would you favor
those who would raze it to throw up a highrise?
Such questions he encountered daily
in water-cooler nooks and offices
that bubbled with gossip about Alger Hiss.
Yet he never forgot that night on the deck and felt infused
with new power. This added to his charm, his growing
dissatisfaction with the limits of the legal
profession. He listened to classical music and thought
how fine it would be to win a land war in Asia.

**5**

If "let me make one thing perfectly clear" was his motto,
could we assume his aim was clarity, if not candor?
Such questions nagged him, too. One day at the White House
he realized what he'd been saying for the past ten minutes
was nonsense, bullshit—and he said so with gusto.
An aide shook his hand and left.
For once the Oval Office was empty.
He wanted to put both feet up on his desk
and say, "Ladies and gentlemen, thanks a lot."
Instead, he strolled past the window, hands clasped behind him,
and made the call to invade Cambodia.

**6**

He put down the phone and stared out the window. Julie's
        wedding
in the Rose Garden would be matched by the funeral of
        Watergate,
the ghost years at San Clemente and Key Biscayne
where the ocean forgave no one.
He would outlive Khruschev and Mao.
He would come into his own. He would rise
above his memoirs as swiftly as he had said good-bye to his
        mentor.
Ike had developed bedsores and called for a nurse,
but he had to get back to the White House, so he said,
"Hey, Ike, did you hear the one about the drunk caddy?"
And when Ike didn't seem to hear,
he said, "So long, fella."

# ANNA'S SONG

By now the Master was deaf and went on working
when I called him to dinner.
He would sit at the piano
and time a sonata
to a game of hide-and-seek
he played with his shadow cast
in candlelight on the carpet.

I would be sweeping or cleaning the keys
in ascending stepladders of sound
when he would crash in scattering
bits of music paper like confetti scribbling
me lovenotes deathnotes notes
about how the music of Handel made him think of linden

rows outside a noisy beerhall
until I swear I could taste beer in those trees
could smell the foam of ale in glasses
raised to the whitewooded branches.
Then he would play something and make me sit
on his tattered sparrow of a couch and call me queen
of the Rhine ignoring my steelgray hair

my face an apron of wrinkles.
And I would listen and it would be the coronation
waltz of the pinetree prince in the mill town
where I was a girl and braided my hair.
*Piggytails* my lover called me long ago pulling
me down on the pineneedles.

I remember peeking out from under the boughs
later trying to look hard
pretending I knew how to smoke
as the sun came up over the waxworks glazing
the chimney pots.
Even then I wanted to cry hosanna
to the pigeons and sing immortal songs.

Even then I knew the sound of legs rubbing
is a miracle of wild hush.
It is the crickets' lullaby to the moonless
shore of a pinetree island
where my lover comes to me
with pipe and timbrel.

# One Two Three Four Five →

# ON LEARNING THE PEOPLE'S REPUBLIC OF CHINA HAS LIFTED ITS BAN ON BEETHOVEN

A million shuttered windows in Shanghai
are opening at this moment onto wall
posters and housing projects.

Uniformed teachers and tradesmen are up
before work tuning radios
in brightening parlors.

Soon the Eroica Symphony lifts off.
Like a giant blue-green insect
iridescent over Nanking Road

it wakes nine million comrades
with the citywide thunder
rumblings of an E flat

it makes by fanning
four net-veined
pagoda-heavy wings.

❋   ❋   ❋

Somewhere between blue and green
at Ellsworth Farm by the dock
where I learned to swim one summer

dragonflies disturbing the shush
of waves against the rushes made me think
of a prop plane's drumroll high

over a rice paddy where men ankle-deep
in ox piss and women balancing baskets
on their heads blended with Adirondack

cattails and marsh grass.
An oarlock popped; I could hear
my sister call our dog across the water,

but nothing mattered
except the pulse and drumroll of E flat
from the Emperor Concerto.

❋　❋　❋

That day on Mott Street with the windows
rolled down to catch a whiff of Peking
duck and bluefish green at the gills

when you shut your eyes and leaned back
against the headrest so that your hair,
pulled tight and straight, looked Oriental

I thought of Ezra Pound at the wheel
of his wicker chair: rattan, I thought, rat-a-tat,
the buzz and clatter of horns

like chopsticks banged on a baby
grand by a boy in a second-floor window.
I thought: "Chinatown streets are so narrow

I could put my feet across
and touch both curbs like a Venetian
Bridge of Sighs."

❋　❋　❋

The wish to write about China
so that nothing distracts the reader
from the fundamental lily

is like the push to procreate
and bring up daughters to believe
a billion people sipping jasmine tea

have sweetened culture from its cradle
with spoonfuls of that black
gunpowder, meditation.

This is the sound of blackness,
the quadrophonic silence of space
when midnight throws cinder

block shadows all over
the Great Wall of China
and will not play moonlight sonatas.

❀  ❀  ❀

Now the fan's eye glues me to its dream
of ice cubes, and I think
of rice paper hand fans unfolding

in formal gardens between evergreen hills
that could be called mountains.
They could be called maestros

of the north wind that beguiles us
and leaves us tranquil in valleys.
Or they could be called catafalques

of Yangtze warlords under sky-
blue pavilions. So what
are we doing in the middle

of summer, listening
to river-sweet
mandarin ramblings?

❀  ❀  ❀

Again nothing matters—nothing buzzes
or clatters—only the humdrum reveille
of days when I feel my chest

cave in pressed down by a paper
tiger, a mood, not a man.
I think of a cadaverous

**57**

coolie stretched
on a bamboo pallet:
among water pipes, sallow as wax,

he puffs all day and hears the freight
train of his future go up in smoke,
concentrating on the belly

button of a manchild marbled
with bronze fat
on a prerevolutionary altar.

❖   ❖   ❖

Junks and sampans are scattering
as Hong Kong harbor darkens
under whitecaps from the South China Sea

and the mainland braces for floods.
Again the bony mountains
surrounding the city are beheaded

by gray clouds,
and the Pastoral Symphony rises
from its nest

of typhoon furies. Listen,
a hundred-headed dragon is slaying a fleet
of trawlers with the whip-

lash of its forked
thunder-echoing
tongues.

# PASSAGE

### 1

Near South Fallsburg the woods thin out.
Broadleaf and evergreen stretches
give way to golf courses and centers for yoga.
Split-levels and rundown farms fit into a puzzle
of secondary growth—stringy Catskill birch,
ailanthus lean and hungry. One thinks of an old
swami rising from lotus position with a wand of peacock
feathers and the promise that out of this muck
of mind, this dumping ground for beer cans and despair,
one might recycle nectar.

### 2

My bliss leaps up like a honey-colored Bengal tiger.
Under a palmyra palm, polishing my stripes
with a sandpaper tongue,
I have dozed for decades in the shade.
I have swallowed the cobra of depression
as well as the mongoose of euphoria.
There is no end to the brush-clad plateau.
There is only the water hole where gazelles gather,
where I have sprung anew
with a sabre-toothed mantra.

### 3

Om. A line of disciples broadens
down a carpeted aisle toward a stage.
Shoeless, from all walks, they carry baskets
of fruit, flowers, or else nickel bags of dope,
whiskey bottles—and their passage over the rug
is marked by the absence of shuffling.
Somewhere elephants with diminutive ears
munch the tender shoots of treetops
and in good time honor night's guru, Death,
by laying down their tusks and trunks quietly.

### 4

Out of the quiet, the windowless
dark, where I have meditated on a mat,
I will come forth chanting.
I will celebrate the fireman killed in Calcutta.
I will put no other gods before his skull
laid low by a brick. I will capture the stink
of a burnt-out storefront blackly. I will catch
the first impressions of his widow
and daughter in saris, pausing over rice,
listening to news on the wireless.

**5**

I will praise the peasant mother
who hitchhiked a thousand kilometers to Delhi
with four children, one an infant on her back,
only to have the authorities tell her
she must return to Ganeshpuri
to fill out more forms
before she could collect one rupee.
I will paint her thin defiant lips.
I will highlight her fine black hair and set
a crimson dot as a seal upon her forehead.

**6**

I will tell you the truth, friends:
Despair is no impostor. He cares not
for our rupees or rank
among beggars. He wears
all turbans and has dined with Krishna.
The bureaucracy of sin, the blind
corridors of religion, are familiar to him.
I tell you, friends,
he leaves work at close of day
like many another slaughtered cow.

**7**

He bikes past a couple of Brahman
bulls unyoked on the road; Hondas
honk, men in Nehru caps
lean out of car windows and jeer in Hindi
while the bulls graze nonplussed, their humps abob.
He pedals past the Portuguese consulate and a lawn
party of British naval officers raising a toast
in honor of Bombay gin. They lift glasses
to the sun as it drops over the Arabian Sea—
ever westward toward London.

**8**

Just so, Despair has vanished into the brush
outside of South Fallsburg. By a bridge
over a spillway, I sat cross-legged on a bench
and shut my eyes. I saw
him coast on his English racer, ashen with fatigue,
into a scrubby grove of birch and ailanthus.
I recall geese honking and the fact
that the lake's name, Nityananda,
kept echoing on my tongue
like curry and coriander.

**9**

I recall glancing up
at an orange-robed swami leading a band
of disciples through a glass-enclosed
walkway toward an auditorium.
The passage was narrow, cramped,
yet they glided by with room to spare—
two of them preceded the swami,
walking backward, chatting with him,
and hefting sitars.
A conch shell blew, and we were summoned in.

**10**

In. Far-reaching Conch Shell whose note
calls forth chariot lines of warriors in the *Gita*
as well as a darshan line, you have summoned me in
from landscapes of distress
to meditate on higher consciousness.
You have lured me away from animal flesh
and the smell of guilt,
which have plagued my people since Noah's monsoon.
Now I put my lips to your mouth and blow
a long low note.

## 11

I, too, am a husk reincarnate.
I, too, am an echo of waves crashing: the Bay
of Bengal sings in my veins.
Dinghies bobbing among supertankers
compose a refrain my pulse and economics know.
I, too, am sounding a call
among boat people of all castes.
Let us launch a pleasure craft
whose only mode of power, sails notwithstanding,
is the intensity of our bliss.

## 12

Ah, Conch Shell, your single note, Om,
recalls a day in Mexico when I went walking
on a beach and bought a conch shell from a street vender
and brought it back to my hotel
balcony and blew, thinking:
Here I am at the Pacific above brown-skinned swimmers.
Then I felt a sudden tremor, a shock
of incense and rosewater,
and saw, laid out before me like a postcard,
ten thousand pilgrims bathing in the Ganges.

# PITT POETRY SERIES

**Ed Ochester, General Editor**